How To Use AI
To Write A Book
To Grow & Scale Your Business
In 90 Days Or Less

Table Of Contents

INTRODUCTION

What Is Ai And How Can It Be Used For Business And Scalability

AI, or artificial intelligence, refers to using machines and algorithms to simulate human cognitive abilities such as perception, reasoning, learning, and decision-making. AI has several uses, from recognizing patterns in data to automating complex tasks.

In business, AI can be used to improve scalability in several ways. Here are a few examples:

◆ **Streamlining operations:** AI can automate routine tasks, freeing human employees to focus on higher-level tasks requiring more creativity and critical thinking. This can help businesses scale their operations without needing to hire additional staff.

◆ **Personalizing customer experiences:** By analyzing data on customer behavior and preferences, AI can help businesses personalize their marketing and sales efforts. This can improve customer engagement and loyalty, increasing sales and revenue.

◆ **Improving decision-making:** AI can examine massive amounts of data and spot trends and patterns that people might not see immediately. This can help businesses make better-informed decisions about everything from supply chain management to product development.

◆ **Enhancing customer service:** AI-powered chatbots and virtual assistants can provide 24/7 support to customers, improving response times and reducing the workload on human customer service representatives.

Understanding The Importance Of Writing A Business Book

Writing a business book can have several benefits for entrepreneurs and business leaders. The following are some factors that make creating a business book necessary:

Establishing thought leadership:

Writing a book can help you establish yourself as an expert. By sharing your knowledge and ideas with others, you might set yourself as an intellectual leader and the go-to person for advice.

Building your brand:

Your brand may grow, and you can become more visible in your sector with the aid of a well-written business book. Additionally, it might aid in bringing in fresh clients, consumers, or company associates.

Generating leads:

A business book can be a powerful lead-generation tool. By offering valuable insights and information in your book, you can attract potential customers or clients interested in your products or services.

Providing value to your audience:

By writing a book, you can give value to your audience beyond what you offer through your business. As a result, your relationships with your clients and consumers will get stronger, increasing brand loyalty.

Leaving a legacy:

Writing a book can have a lasting impact on your industry and share your knowledge with future generations. It might serve as a means of chronicling your development as a business owner or executive.

The 90-Day Timeline And Why It Matters

It can be a potent approach to expand and scale your business to use AI to create a book, but having a clear timeline and plan is essential. A 90-day timeline can be an effective way to stay on track and ensure you can complete your book quickly and efficiently.
Here are a few reasons why a 90-day timeline matters:

- **It helps you stay focused:** Writing a book can be daunting, and it's easy to get overwhelmed or lose focus. A 90-day timeline can help you break the process into manageable chunks and stay on track.
- **It creates a sense of urgency:** A 90-day deadline makes a sense of urgency and can keep you motivated while you're writing. It also ensures you can complete your book quickly and start reaping the benefits immediately.
- **It helps you prioritize:** When you have limited time to write a book, you must plan how to spend it. A 90-day timeline can help you prioritize your tasks and focus on the most critical aspects of your book.
- **It ensures that your book is timely:** Writing a book requires a substantial time and financial commitment, so it must be current and valuable when published. A 90-day timeline can help you write a book addressing current industry trends and issues.

Overall, a 90-day timeline can effectively use AI to write a book that grows and scales your business. By staying focused, creating a sense of urgency, prioritizing your tasks, and ensuring that your book is timely, you can make a high-quality book quickly.

CHAPTER 1
DEFINING YOUR BUSINESS GOALS

A business goal is an endpoint, accomplishment, or target an organization wants to achieve in the short or long term. Business goals can take many different forms and be aspirational or motivational, such as driving an organization toward a specific objective like improved customer service. They can also have clear objectives, such as reaching a particular revenue target, net income, profit margin, profit goal, or other financial milestone.

A mission statement is often seen as the definition of an organization's purpose and reason to exist, which is a form of a business goal. A vision statement is another common way for an organization to articulate its goals by providing an outlook on where it wants to go.

Why Are Business Goals Important?

Business goals are essential for numerous reasons affecting an organization's overall operations and success.

Business goals help measure progress. Business goals provide the milestones that can help an organization measure its success or lack thereof.

Business goals set the direction of a company. Business objectives provide all personnel with a clear understanding of the direction and end state of the organization.

Business goals establish accountability. Business goals enable management to take ownership of its successes or failures.

Business goals improve decision-making. Business goals align the activities of the business so management can constantly evaluate decisions to ensure the industry moves toward its target.

Setting clear and achievable goals: Setting clear and achievable goals is critical for the success of any business or project. Here are some crucial actions to define precise, doable goals:

Start with a vision: It's critical to clearly understand your objectives before setting any precise targets. Your image should be inspiring and motivate you to take action.

Make your goals specific: Specific goals are easier to measure and track progress. Clearly state your objectives and then divide them into manageable, quantifiable steps.

Use the SMART framework: The SMART framework is a valuable tool for setting goals that are specific, measurable, attainable, relevant, and time-bound. Your objectives may be made more possible and practical with the aid of this framework.

Set deadlines: Setting deadlines can help you stay focused and motivated to achieve your goals. Based on their significance and possible influence on your company, it is crucial to prioritize them. This will enable you to prioritize your goals and keep your efforts directed toward them...

Prioritize your goals: It's crucial to rank them according to their significance and possible influence on your company. By doing so, you'll be able to focus your efforts and ensure you're working toward the most crucial objectives.

Break down significant goals into smaller milestones: You can stay motivated and monitor your progress toward your larger objective by breaking big plans into smaller, achievable milestones.

Regularly review and adjust your plans: If necessary, frequently check your goals to ensure they match your business strategy and priorities.

Developing a plan: Developing a plan is essential for any business or project to succeed. Here are some crucial actions to do to create an efficient method:

Establish your goals: Start by outlining your objectives in detail.
What do you want to achieve? Your objectives should be specific, measurable, and achievable. Conducting a SWOT analysis can assist you in determining the advantages, disadvantages, opportunities, and threats facing your company in your objectives. This analysis can help you identify areas of your business that need improvement and potential growth opportunities.

Establish your target market's identity: Who are your consumers or clients? Determine their wants, likes, and habits to customize your plan to meet their needs. Develop strategies based on your SWOT analysis and target audience to achieve your objectives. These strategies should be specific, actionable, and realistic.

Create a strategy

Make an action plan that details the precise steps to carry out your intentions. This plan should include timelines, milestones, and metrics for measuring progress.

Set a budget

Determine the resources required to implement your project and set a budget that aligns with your goals and financial capabilities.

Assign responsibilities:

Assign specific duties to team members and stakeholders, including timelines for completion.

4Monitor and adjust: Track your progress toward your goals and make any required revisions to maintain your plan aligned with your business strategy and priorities.

Identifying Where Ai Can Be Applied To Accelerate Results

Identifying where AI can be applied to accelerate results requires a thorough understanding of the business processes and areas where automation can bring the most value. Here are some common areas where AI can be applied to accelerate results:

Client service: Chatbots and virtual assistants powered by AI can respond to basic client questions and offer tailored suggestions based on user behavior, cutting down on wait times and boosting customer satisfaction.

Sales and Marketing: AI can help identify and target potential customers with personalized marketing messages and recommendations. It can also analyze sales data to identify patterns and predict future sales trends.

Operations and Logistics: AI can optimize supply chain management, predict demand, and optimize inventory levels to reduce waste and streamline processes.

Quality Control and Maintenance: AI can help identify defects and patterns in quality control processes, reducing waste and improving product quality. It can also predict maintenance needs and schedule repairs before equipment fails.

Human Resources: By automating time-consuming chores like interview scheduling and resume screening, AI may free up HR professionals' time to work on more critical projects.

Finance: AI can analyze financial data and provide predictive analytics, identifying potential risks and opportunities for cost savings and revenue growth.

Businesses can accelerate results and improve efficiency by identifying areas where AI can be applied, freeing time and resources for more strategic initiatives. First, however, it's essential to carefully evaluate AI implementation's potential benefits and risks and ensure that the technology aligns with the business's overall strategy and goals.

CHAPTER 2
HOW DO YOU FIND YOUR UNIQUE ANGLE FROM PRODUCTS TO SERVICES ON THE WEB

Identifying Your Niche:

The Internet has become a valuable information and purchasing tool for today's consumers. Virtually everything can be researched online, and you can browse the best items and discounts from the comfort of your home, anytime you choose.

Mail-order enterprises are expanding as well for some of the same factors, as customers discover better deals from businesses that don't have the expense of a storefront.

Consumers today have access to everything. Thus, the proprietor of a home company may profit from this market culture. In addition, business owners may do business in the comfort of their homes, just as customers can purchase from their living rooms and kitchens. Therefore, starting a home company can be ideal if you want to set your hours, spend less time commuting, and benefit from the overall freedom of working for yourself.

Spending time identifying your specialization is a critical component of your first home business development strategy.

So what does "finding your niche" actually mean? Finding a niche in customer interest and capitalizing on it are critical components of location identification. Finding a place in the corporate sector is necessary to stand out. For example, hundreds of bookstores may exist, but how many specialize in the books that interest you specifically? You can face competition from hundreds of other book vendors if your home-based business is focused on book sales. However, you could find yourself in direct competition with fewer enterprises if your home-based business is primarily focused on selling books on outdoor activities.

How do you determine your specialty now that you are aware of one? Start by posing a few crucial questions to yourself.

What Skills Do I Have?

Make a list of every ability you possess. Do you have good mechanical skills? Do you have a talent for decorating? Do all of your friends turn to you for computer support? Do you genuinely understand all there is to know about a particular subject? List the abilities you already have in each category. You might be surprised by where your talents lie.

What Do I Enjoy Doing?

What pastimes do you find so fulfilling that you would participate in them even if there were a chance of financial gain? The most excellent place to start when answering this question is by looking at your hobbies. These are frequent activities that cost substantial money to participate in. So why not do so? Launching a home company may take a lot of time and work, so finding a love for your industry can be a fantastic source of the perseverance required to get through the initial challenges.

What Is The Purpose Of This?

It's time to consider the market for these items when you list your strengths and passions. For example, are you always looking for supplies for your hobby but need help finding what you need? Others likely have the same difficulty, and this market segment would receive a home business that supplies this need.

You can follow the methods listed below to find your niche:

- **Define your skills and expertise:** Start by defining your skills and expertise. What are you good at? Which abilities or experiences do you are equipped with that distinguish you from others?
- **Identify your passions:** Think about what you're passionate about. What topics or areas do you enjoy working on? What do you find most fulfilling?
- **Research your industry:** Look at your industry and identify underserved or overlooked areas. What gaps or unmet needs could you address with your skills and expertise?
- **Consider your target audience:** Consider who your target audience is and their specific needs and pain points. What solutions can you offer to help address those needs?
- **Test and refine:** Test different niches with your target audience to see what resonates best. Use feedback to refine and hone your approach.

Standing Out In A Crowded Market

Gaining an advantage over your rivals can be difficult, and getting your company noticeable in a competitive market is much more difficult. Standing out is essential for survival, whether you have a novel concept for a crowded market or are an early adopter observing a weed-like growth in the competition. If you want your company to stand out in all the right ways, we offer a few suggestions to get you started.

It may be difficult to stand out in a crowded market, but there are a number of strategies you may use to distinguish yourself from your competitors:

Identify your unique value proposition:

Your distinctive value proposition distinguishes you from your rivals and makes you special. It could be your expertise, approach, pricing, or customer service. Whatever it is, ensure it's straightforward for your target audience to understand.

Focus on your target audience:

Understand your target audience's problems and who they are. Develop a deep understanding of their needs, wants, and desires, and tailor your messaging and marketing efforts accordingly.

Offer exceptional customer service:

Excellent customer service can be a crucial differentiator in a crowded market. Ensure you're responsive, empathetic, and helpful to your customers at every touchpoint.

Leverage social proof:

The concept of social proof holds that individuals arelikelier to trust and buy from a business others have already used and recommended. Use customer reviews, testimonials, Use case studies to establish credibility with your target audience and demonstrate social proof.

Embrace innovation and creativity:

Look for new and innovative ways to differentiate yourself from your competitors. Experiment with new marketing channels, offer unique products or services or develop creative messaging and branding that stands out.

Collaborate with others:

Working together with other companies or influential people in your sector may expand your audience and increase your credibility.

Remember, standing out in a crowded market takes time and effort, but it's worth it. You may establish a devoted following and succeed over the long run by standing out from the competition and providing outstanding value to your target audience.

The Importance Of Authenticity In Business Storytelling

Humans are a storytelling species. We have always used stories to express ourselves and understand the world. As a result, it shouldn't come as a surprise if the businesses that master story also stand out from the competitors. As consumers, we support brands aligning with our values and inspiring us to act. We interact with companies that both educate and amuse us. And we stick with companies that make us the protagonist of their stories.

Brand storytelling has changed from taglines and billboards to a dynamic, two-way discussion between businesses and companies and their clients in the era of online communication and content marketing. In order to convey compelling tales and build a genuine community, it is imperative to comprehend this transformation.

Authenticity in business storytelling is essential for building trust and connecting with your audience. Here are some reasons why authenticity is vital in business storytelling:

Builds trust:

Authentic storytelling helps build trust with your audience by showing that you are genuine and transparent. When you share stories that are true to your brand and values, your audience will likely trust you and develop a deeper connection with your business.

Establishes a connection:

By demonstrating your understanding of your audience's needs, wants, and desires, authentic storytelling aids in building a rapport with them. When you share stories that resonate with your audience, they are likelier to see you as a relatable and trustworthy partner.

Differentiate your brand:

Authentic storytelling can help differentiate your brand from competitors. By sharing stories unique to your brand and values, you can stand out in a crowded market and establish yourself as a leader in your industry.

Drives engagement:

Authentic storytelling can drive engagement by creating an emotional connection with your audience. When you share relatable stories that resonate with individuals are more inclined to interact with your brand than your audience, share your content, and become loyal customers.

Inspires action:

Authentic storytelling can inspire action by showing your audience how your brand positively impacts the world. They are more likely to back your company and assist in spreading your message when you offer tales that reflect the values of your audience and motivate them to act.

Remember, authenticity in business storytelling is not about being perfect or polished. It's about being true to your brand and values and sharing stories that resonate with your audience. You can build trust, establish a connection, and inspire action with your audience by being authentic in your storytelling.

CHAPTER 3
MARKET RESEARCH AND GATHERING DATA

Market research and gathering data are essential components of any successful business strategy. By understanding your customers, competitors, and industry trends, you may decide based on information that promotes development and profitability.

Market research and data gathering begin by defining your research objectives. For example, what questions do you want to answer? What facts are necessary for you to make wise decisions? By specifying your research objectives, you can focus your efforts and ensure your research is relevant and actionable.

Once you have defined your research objectives, The next step is figuring out who your market of choice is. What are the requirements, wants, and preferences of your customers? Again, a deep understanding of your target audience's demographics, psychographics, and behaviors is essential for effective market research.

Many different research methods include surveys, focus groups, interviews, and secondary research. The best strategy will depend on your study objectives and target audience. Each method has benefits and drawbacks.

Surveys are a standard research method and involve asking a series of questions to a large sample of people. Surveys are a valuable tool for gathering data in quantitative form on a wide range of subjects and can be carried out online, over the phone, or in person. Ensuring that your survey questions are precise, concise, and pertinent to your research goals is the key to creating effective surveys.

Focus groups are another popular research method and involve bringing together a small group to discuss a specific topic or issue. Focus groups are valuable for gathering in-depth information on consumer attitudes, beliefs, and actions. The key to conducting influential focus groups is ensuring you have a clear agenda, a skilled facilitator, and diverse participants.

Interviews are a more in-depth research method involving one-on-one conversations with customers or industry experts. Interviews are an effective way to gather detailed information on specific topics or issues. The key to conducting compelling interviews is ensuring you have a clear agenda, an open-minded approach, and a skilled interviewer.

Secondary research involves gathering data from existing sources, such as industry reports, competitor websites, and government databases. Secondary research may be a valuable tool for swiftly and affordably collecting data. The key to conducting effective secondary research is to ensure that you use reputable sources and that your data is relevant and up-to-date.

The following phase is data analysis after data collection. Take note of any patterns, trends, or insights that might assist in guiding your company decisions. Consider using data visualization tools like charts and graphs to help make sense of your data.

Finally, use your research insights to inform your business decisions. Whether you're launching a new product, developing a marketing strategy, or making operational changes, use your data to guide your choices and ensure that you're meeting the needs of your target audience.

Conducting Thorough Research And Analysis

Any firm that wants to make wise judgments and remain competitive must do in-depth research and analysis. You may find growth possibilities, reduce risks, and make strategic decisions that advance your business by collecting and evaluating data about your clients, rivals, and market trends.

The first step in conducting thorough research and analysis is to define your research objectives. What questions do you want to answer? What facts are necessary for you to make wise decisions? By clearly defining your research objectives, you can ensure that your research efforts are focused and relevant to your business needs.

The next step is to determine your data sources. You can acquire various data kinds, including primary data (which you independently obtain) and secondary data (maintained by others).

Preliminary data can be gathered through surveys, focus groups, and interviews, while secondary data can be obtained from government databases, industry reports, and competitor websites. You must gather and evaluate your data after identifying your data sources. Data analysis involves examining your data to identify patterns, trends, and insights that can help inform your business decisions. This may include using statistical software to analyze your data or creating visual representations of your data, such as graphs or charts.

Using reliable and valid data sources is essential when conducting research and analysis. This means ensuring your data is accurate, up-to-date, and relevant to your research objectives. In addition, it would be advantageous to consider further the constraints placed on the data-gathering process or any biases in your data sources.

One effective way to conduct research and analysis is through competitive intelligence. Competitive intelligence involves gathering information on your competitors, such as their products and services, pricing strategies, and marketing tactics. You may find possibilities for your company to stand out from other businesses and grow by examining their advantages and disadvantages.

In addition to competitive intelligence, you should also gather data on your customers. This includes data on customer demographics, psychographics, and behaviors, as well as their needs, wants, and preferences. By understanding your customers, You may build services and goods that cater to their demands and marketing strategies specifically designed to appeal to them.

Finally, reviewing and updating your research and analysis regularly is essential. Business conditions and market trends can change quickly, and staying up-to-date on the latest developments is crucial for making informed decisions. As a result, you may remain ahead of the competition and set up your company for long-term success by regularly examining and upgrading your research and analysis.

Using Ai Tools To Gather And Analyze Data

Artificial intelligence (AI) tools can gather and analyze data more efficiently and effectively than traditional methods. Large amounts of data can be processed fast and correctly by AI-powered systems, which may also find patterns and insights that people would not immediately see.

Web scraping software is one example of an AI tool for data gathering and analysis. Web scraping involves automatically extracting data from websites and other online sources. This can include data on competitors, industry trends, customer reviews, etc. Using web scraping tools; businesses can gather large volumes of data quickly and efficiently and use this data to inform their decision-making.

Another AI tool for data analysis is machine learning algorithms. Machine learning is analyzing data and making predictions based on that data using statistical models and algorithms. For instance, companies may employ machine learning algorithms to forecast client behavior, spot patterns in sales data, or enhance marketing initiatives.

Another AI technology that may be used to collect and evaluate data is natural language processing (NLP). NLP entails teaching machines to comprehend human language, which may be used to assess social media postings, consumer reviews, and other unstructured data sources. For example, businesses can use NLP to identify customer sentiment, track brand mentions, and gain additional insights from unstructured data sources that may require more manual work.

One potential challenge with using AI tools for data gathering and analysis is ensuring the accuracy and reliability of the data. This is so because the insights produced by AI algorithms may need to be corrected if the information provided for training them is biased or inaccurate. Therefore, organizations must ensure that their data sources are trustworthy and utilize the proper techniques for data cleansing and validation.

Overall, AI tools can be a powerful way for businesses to gather and analyze data and help identify patterns and insights that may take time to be apparent using traditional methods. In addition, by using AI tools in conjunction with other research and analysis methods, businesses can gain a complete understanding of their customers, competitors, and market trends. With the use of this knowledge, they may make more sensible and sensible business judgments.

CHAPTER 4
CREATING AN OUTLINE

When composing a piece of writing, you often create an outline before writing the actual content of the work. Outlines help develop your ideas, organize your details, and assist in revisions. Creating an effective outline can help you improve your writing and produce a better piece.

What Is An Outline?

An outline is a helpful tool to help you arrange your thoughts when explaining ideas. Whether you are drafting a speech, writing a novel, or trying to share ideas for a book report, an outline is a well-structured document highlighting key points and opinions you want to convey.

Writing a comprehensive and effective outline requires critical thinking to identify and select key points of your topic. It also requires adherence to format and strategic brevity. Outlines are high-level documents that typically start off a project or offer important insight. For these reasons, all varieties of organizations and institutions work with outlines. They are important for people specializing in communications or any field where communication is essential.

Organizing Your Thoughts & Ideas

Organizing your thoughts and ideas is essential in any writing or creative process. You may need a clear framework and strategy to stay focused and accomplish your goals.

Here are some tips for organizing your thoughts and ideas:

Start with a brainstorming session:

Write it down no matter how little or large an idea may appear. You can use a mind map, sticky notes, or a simple list to capture your ideas. This can help you get all your thoughts out of your head and onto paper.

Group your ideas into themes:

Look for patterns and connections in your thoughts and group them into themes or categories. This helps you get a broad perspective and locate essential issues you wish to investigate in your writing.

Create an outline:

Construct a plan for your writing endeavor once your themes have been determined. Depending on your preferences, this might be a broad overview or a specific strategy. Your writing will be planned and ordered if you use an outline to keep you on track.

Use technology to stay organized:

You can keep organized and on schedule with various tools. For example, you may use project management software, note-taking applications, or a straightforward spreadsheet to keep track of your thoughts and developments.

Take breaks:

Pausing and occasionally moving away from your work is crucial. Doing this lets you relax and return to your task with new insight. Use this time to put your thoughts and ideas into order, or relax and refuel.

Though it might take some time, organizing your thoughts and ideas is essential if you want to succeed. You can set yourself up for success and ensure that your writing is focused and organized by taking the time to brainstorm, arrange your thoughts into topics, write an outline, use technology to keep organized, and take pauses.

How To Structure Your Book For Maxim Impact:

Structuring your book is a crucial part of the writing process, as it can significantly impact the effectiveness and impact of your message. A well-structured book can keep readers engaged, make your writing memorable, and effectively convey your message. Here are some tips for structuring your text for maximum impact:

Before starting to write, it is essential to identify the objective of your work and the intended readership. This will assist you in organizing your book such that it appeals to your target readership and conveys your point. Consider the subject of your book, your goals, and the profile of your ideal reader.

Create an outline:

Outlining your book is the next step after deciding your aim and target audience. You should structure your thoughts and ideas and make your workflow logical using an outline. Your book's essential parts and chapters and any subheadings or important topics you wish to emphasize should be included.

Start with an engaging introduction:

The introduction is your chance to hook your readers and draw them into your book. It should be attention-grabbing, clear, and concise. Describe the subject of your book and why readers should care. It would be best if you opened with a tale, a startling statistic, or a thought-provoking comment.

Use a consistent structure:

Use a consistent format inside each chapter or section of your book to make it simple for readers to follow along. For example, start each chapter with an overview, followed by several sub-sections, and then end with a conclusion. A consistent structure makes your book more accessible and easier to navigate.

Include examples and stories:

Use examples and tales to demonstrate your views and make your writing more interesting. They can also make your message more memorable to readers. Be sure to include examples and stories relevant to your target audience and reinforcing your overall message.

End with a firm conclusion:

The conclusion is your chance to summarize your key points and leave readers with a clear call to action. It must be memorable, compelling and leave readers wondering what they should do next. Consider ending with a special quote, a powerful statement, or a summary of your main message.

Consider design and formatting:

The design and formatting of your book can also impact its impact. Consider using subheadings, bullet points, and other style strategies to make your work more readable. Additionally, consider your book's cover design and overall visual appeal, as these factors can influence readers' first impressions.

Mapping Out Chapters And Subsections

To create a compelling tale that is enjoyable to write and read, a novelist must consider characters, storylines, landscapes, points of view, and fantastical aspects. You should think more carefully about the structure of your novel as a result. Of course, paying attention to your book's technical and structural elements is easy. But is the structure of your story important anyway?

Absolutely! Every technical element feeds into your storytelling, from chapter to punctuation to sentence length.

Organizing your thoughts and establishing a clear framework for your book using chapter and subsection maps is essential to the writing process. The following advice will help you successfully organize the chapters and subdivisions of your book:

Start with your outline:

Before you can map out your book's chapters and subsections, you must have a solid outline. Your outline should include the main sections of your book and the key points you want to make in each area. Once you have a thorough overview, you may begin organizing it into chapters and subsections.

Group-related content:

Look for ways to group-related content. This will help you create coherent chapters that flow logically and make sense to readers. Suppose you're producing a marketing book, for instance. In that case, you may divide the chapters into categories depending on the many marketing channels you'll use, such as social media, email marketing, and content marketing.

Use subheadings:

Use subheadings to divide up the text and make each chapter simpler to read. The subheadings, which should be clear and comprehensive, should be able to inform readers of what they may anticipate learning in each section.

Consider the length of each chapter:

Think about the ideal size for each chapter. Chapters that are too long can overwhelm readers, while too short chapters can feel incomplete. Aim for chapters that are roughly the same length, and that can be read in one sitting.

Ensure a logical flow:

As you map out your chapters and subsections, ensure a logical flow from one section to the next. Your book should feel cohesive, with each chapter building on the previous one.

Edit and revise:

Take the time to edit and make changes when you have a draft of your book's chapters and subsections. Look for ways to tighten the structure, eliminate redundancies, and make the content flow more smoothly. For example, you may need to reorganize chapters or combine sections to create a more cohesive structure.You may develop a clear and cogent structure that makes it simple for readers to follow along and comprehend your content by outlining your book's chapters and subsections. A well-structured book can help you connect with your target audience, convey your message effectively, and ultimately achieve your writing goals.

CHAPTER 5
WRITING YOUR BOOK

A step-by-step guide can help new authors overcome the intimidating parts of writing a book, allowing them to stay focused and maximize their creativity.

Writing an entire book can be a daunting task, especially for new writers. It requires hard work, extreme ambition, and intense discipline. Even for successful writers of bestsellers, the hardest part of the writing process can be simply sitting down to write the first page. If you take it one step at a time, though, writing a book is an attainable goal.

Develop A Writing System That Works For You

For your writing process to remain reliable and productive, you must create a method that works for you. The following stages will assist you in developing a unique writing system:

Assess your writing preferences:

Reflect on your preferred writing environment, time of day, and tools. Some writers thrive in a quiet space, while others find inspiration in bustling cafes. Determine whether you prefer to write in the morning, afternoon, or evening. Consider whether you prefer pen and paper or digital tools for writing.

Establish a writing routine:

Consistency is critical to developing a writing habit. Set aside dedicated time for writing each day or week. Create a schedule that aligns with your lifestyle and commitments. Whether it's early morning, during lunch breaks, or evenings, find a routine that works best for you.

Define your goals and objectives:

Clearly define your writing goals and objectives. Are you working towards completing a specific word count or finishing a chapter? Setting tangible goals helps keep you focused and motivated. Break larger goals into smaller, achievable milestones.

Plan and outline your writing projects:

Before diving into writing, plan and outline your projects. This helps provide structure and guidance for your writing process. Outline chapters, sections, or key ideas you want to cover. Having a roadmap makes it easier to stay on track and avoid writer's block.

Use productivity techniques:

Experiment with different styles to enhance your writing process. For example, the Pomodoro Technique involves working for a set amount of time (e.g., 25 minutes) and taking short breaks in between. This helps maintain focus and combat distractions.

Minimize distractions:

Identify and minimize potential distractions during your writing sessions. Disable notifications on your phone, dismiss tabs that aren't essential on your computer and designate a location where you can write without interruptions. Consider using productivity apps or website blockers to stay focused.

Embrace your writing style:

Find and embrace a style that suits you. Some writers prefer to write freely and then revise, while others prefer to edit as they go. Experiment and find a process that allows your creativity to flow while maintaining the quality of your writing.

Seek accountability and support:

Share your writing goals with others and seek accountability. Join writing groups, participate in workshops, or find a writing buddy to provide feedback and support. Being part of a community can keep you motivated and provide valuable insights.

Take breaks and rest:

Writing can be mentally and physically demanding. Remember to take regular intervals and give yourself time to rest and recharge. By taking a break from your job, you can obtain new insights and come back to it with more creativity.

Adapt and refine your system:

As you progress, regularly assess and refine your writing system to align with your evolving needs and goals. Be open to experimenting with new techniques or approaches that may enhance your productivity and creativity.

Creating a personalized writing system takes time and experimentation. Continuously adapt and refine your process to find what works best for you. Remember that everyone's writing journey is unique, so embrace your individuality and enjoy the process of developing your writing system.

Stay On Track With Daily Writing Goals

Staying on track with daily writing goals is essential for completing your book promptly. The following tactics can assist you in keeping up your writing flow:

Set specific daily writing goals:

Break down your writing goals into specific, achievable daily targets. For example, aim to write 500 words each day. Having a clear plan helps keep you motivated and focused.

Create a schedule:

Schedule your writing time each day, and treat it as a non-negotiable appointment. Be realistic about how much effort you can give to writing, and plan your sessions to fit in with other commitments.

Use a timer:

Use a timer to keep track of your writing sessions. Decide how long you'll write for, and try to stay on task. The Pomodoro Technique, which entails working for a certain period (often 25 minutes) and taking brief pauses, is something to think about.

Eliminate distractions:

Minimize distractions during your writing sessions. Please locate a quiet area to write in, put your phone on mute or off, and shut any tabs that aren't required. Consider using noise-canceling headphones or a white noise app to drown out distractions.

Track your progress:

Keep track of your daily word count or writing time. Seeing your progress can be motivating, and it helps you stay on track toward your overall writing goals.

Hold yourself accountable:

Hold yourself responsible for meeting your daily writing goals. To improve accountability, discuss your goals with a friend or writing group. You can also use a productivity app or website that tracks your writing progress and sends reminders to keep you on track.

Celebrate your progress:

Celebrate your daily writing achievements, no matter how small they may seem. Recognize that each word you write brings you closer to completing your book. Celebrating your progress helps keep you motivated and excited about your writing.

Leveraging Ai Tools For Writing, Editing & Proofreading

In recent years, AI-powered tools have become increasingly popular for writers, editors, and proofreaders. These technologies employ machine learning and natural language processing to assist authors in creating better, more understandable work. Here are some ways that AI tools can be leveraged for writing, editing, and proofreading:

Writing:

AI tools can help writers generate ideas, outline their work, and suggest sentence structure and wording. Some popular writing tools that use AI include Grammarly, ProWritingAid, and Hemingway Editor.

Editing:

AI tools can be used to analyze and improve written work's clarity, coherence, and tone. They can also help writers identify errors, such as grammar and spelling. Some AI editing tools include Editage, PaperBlazer, and Ginger Software.

Proofreading:

AI tools can help writers identify and correct errors in written work, such as typos and punctuation errors. Some proofreading tools that use AI include Scribens, Grammarly, and Reverso.

Language Translation:

AI tools can also be used for language translation. They translate texts from one language to another using neural networks, which are used to learn linguistic patterns. Some language translation tools that use AI include Google Translate, DeepL, and Babylon.

AI-powered tools can be handy for writers, editors, and proofreaders. They can help improve the quality and clarity of written work, save time, and reduce the need for human editing and proofreading. However, it's crucial to remain aware that these technologies are flawed and liable for errors. Therefore, it's always a good idea to double-check the suggestions made by AI tools and to use your judgment when making edits or revisions.

CHAPTER 6
DESIGNING YOUR BOOK

Designing your book is an essential aspect of the book creation process that should be noticed. A well-designed book can enhance your audience's reading experience and increase your work's perceived value.

One of the most essential elements of book design is the book cover. Potential readers will notice and be enticed by a visually appealing body to take up your book. Therefore, investing in a professionally designed cover that reflects the content of your book and stands out among the competition is essential.

Another aspect of book design to consider is the typography. The text's font, size, and spacing can significantly affect your book's readability and overall look. Pick a typeface that fits your book's genre and tone while still being simple to read. Use proper spacing and margins to ensure a comfortable reading experience.

Finally, consider incorporating visual elements such as images, illustrations, or graphs to break up the text and add visual interest to your book. However, be careful not to overload your reader with too many visuals that may distract from the content.

CHAPTER 7
EDITING & REVISIONS

Revising and editing are the tasks you undertake to improve your essay significantly. Both are essential elements of the writing process. A finished first draft indicates that only minor revisions are required. Even seasoned writers, meanwhile, need to make edits and revisions to their first versions. Athletes occasionally miss receptions, lose balls, or overshoot goals, as you may be aware. Dancers must recall their steps or risk missing beats or turning too slowly. For both athletes and dancers, the more they practice, the stronger their performance will become. Similar to this, web designers look for better graphics, a cleverer layout, or an eye-catching background for their online pages. Writing may benefit from editing and enhancement in the same way.

Understanding The Purpose Of Revising And Editing

By separating the two critical components of your work during revision and editing, you can give each task your entire focus.

- When you revise, you consider your thoughts again. You could add, remove, shift, or modify certain pieces of information to make your ideas more precise, correct, compelling, or intriguing.
- When you edit, you go back and review your thoughts' expressions. You modify or add words. You correct any grammatical, punctuational, and sentence structural issues. Your writing style develops. Your essay becomes a well-written, mature piece of writing due to your finest efforts.

Creating Unity And Coherence

By strictly following your outline, you can ensure that your writing stays on the subject and does not deviate from the core idea. However, authors' work could end up being less than they intended when they are pressed for time, exhausted, or unable to find the appropriate words. They could have lost the ability to write clearly and succinctly, and they might need to include more details to develop the primary point. When a piece of writing is cohesive, every concept in every paragraph and across the whole essay is expressed with clarity and is ordered in a way that makes sense. The thoughts flow easily when the writing is coherent. The phrasing shows how one concept flows into the next, inside and between paragraphs.

Creating Unity

Sometimes authors become engrossed in the present and find it difficult to resist a pleasant diversion. When talking with friends, you could even like these diversions, but they frequently detract from a piece of writing. When writing her essay's three body paragraphs, which she provisionally named "Digital Technology: The Newest and the Best at What Price?" Mariah adhered closely to her framework. However, a recent HDTV buying excursion disturbed her so much that she strayed from the subject of her third paragraph and made remarks about the salespeople she encountered. She removed the off-topic sentences and disrupted the section's flow when she edited her essay.

Being Clear And Concise

When writing a first draft, some authors are comprehensive and meticulous. Other authors use many words to explain all they feel is necessary to communicate. Which of these writing approaches most closely like your own? Or do you write in a manner that falls somewhere in between? Whichever definition best describes you, the initial draft of practically every piece of writing, regardless of who wrote it, can be made more precise and shorter. Search for superfluous words if you prefer to write excessively. Find particular terms to replace any overly general terminology if your writing tends to be hazy or unclear.

CHAPTER 8
PUBLISHING YOUR BOOK

After you have written and designed your book, it's time to think about publishing. Here are some crucial actions to take into account before releasing your book:

Decide on your publishing route:

There are two main options for publishing your book - traditional or self-publishing. Traditional publishing involves submitting your manuscript to publishing houses that will handle your book's editing, design, and marketing. Self-publishing, on the other hand, consists in taking on these tasks yourself and publishing your book through online platforms like Amazon.

Edit and proofread:

Before publishing your book, thoroughly edit and proofread the content to ensure it is error-free and polished. Consider hiring a professional editor or using online tools like Grammarly to catch any grammar or spelling errors.

Format your book:

Depending on your chosen publishing route, you may need to format your book to meet specific guidelines. This includes formatting the text, adding a table of contents, and including any necessary images or graphics.

Choose a book title and blurb:

Your book title and blurb are essential marketing tools that will help attract potential readers. Please write a brief blurb highlighting your book's main aspects and select a title appropriately describing its content.

Market your book:

Once it is published, promoting it to your target audience is essential. This might entail setting up a website or social media account, launching marketing initiatives, and requesting book reviews.

Traditional Publishing Vs Self-Publishing

Regarding publishing a book, there are two main options: traditional and self-publishing.

In the traditional publishing model, you send your manuscript to a publishing house, and they take care of your book's editing, design, printing, and distribution. Usually, traditional publishers will provide authors with advance payment and ongoing royalties based on book sales. Traditional publishers also have established relationships with bookstores and other retailers, which can help get your book into the hands of more readers.

Self-publishing, on the other hand, involves the responsibilities of editing, designing, printing, and marketing your book. Self-publishing platforms like Amazon's Kindle Direct Publishing and IngramSpark make it relatively easy for authors to get their books published and distributed online. With self-publishing, authors have complete creative control over their work and can earn a higher percentage of royalties per book sold.

Each publishing route has its pros and cons. Traditional publishing can provide a certain level of prestige and validation, as well as access to publishing industry professionals who can help improve the quality of your work. However, the traditional publishing process can be lengthy, with authors often waiting months or years to get a book deal. Traditional publishers may also expect authors to change their work to fit specific marketing or editorial parameters.

Self-publishing allows authors to maintain control over their work and to publish on their timelines. Self-publishing also gives authors a more significant percentage of royalties per book sold, making it a potentially more lucrative option. However, self-publishing can be challenging and time-consuming, with authors responsible for all aspects of the publishing process, including editing, design, and marketing.

Ultimately, the decision between traditional and self-publishing will depend on an author's goals, resources, and preferences. However, both options have the potential to be successful, and it's essential to carefully consider each before making a decision.

Utilizing Ai Tools For Book Marketing And Distribution

Recently, AI tools have become increasingly helpful for book marketing and distribution. Here are some ways in which authors can use AI to help promote and distribute their books:

Social Media Advertising:

Authors may target particular demographics and interests using AI-driven advertising tools on platforms like Facebook, Instagram, and Twitter. Using these tools will enable authors to reach a larger and more targeted audience for their books.

Amazon Ads:

Amazon's advertising platform, Amazon Advertising, allows authors to run ads for their books on Amazon.com. This platform uses AI algorithms to optimize ad targeting, placement, and bidding.

Email Marketing:

AI-driven email marketing platforms like Mailchimp and Campaign Monitor can help authors create targeted email campaigns to promote their books to readers who have expressed interest in similar titles.

Book Discovery Platforms:

Websites like Goodreads and BookBub use AI algorithms to recommend books to readers based on their reading history and preferences. By listing their text on these platforms and optimizing their metadata and keywords, authors can increase their chances of being discovered by potential readers.

Distribution Optimization:

AI tools like Reedsy's Book Editor can help authors optimize their book's metadata and keywords to improve its visibility on online marketplaces like Amazon, Barnes & Noble, and Kobo.

Book Cover Design:

AI tools like Canva and Adobe Spark can help authors create professional-looking book covers optimized for online sales and marketing.

Predictive Analytics:

AI-driven predictive analytics tools can help authors identify the most effective marketing channels and strategies for their book based on data like reader demographics, sales history, and engagement rates.

By leveraging AI tools and platforms for book marketing and distribution, authors can increase their visibility, reach a wider audience, and boost their book sales and success.

CHAPTER 9
LEVERAGING YOUR BOOK FOR BUSINESS GROWTH

A book may be a potent instrument for business expansion. Here are some ways in which authors can leverage their books to grow their business:

Establish Thought Leadership:

Writing a book on a topic related to your business can establish you as a thought leader in your industry. This can increase your credibility and visibility, leading to new business opportunities and partnerships.

Generate Leads:

You can collect leads and build your email list by offering a free chapter or other exclusive content related to your book. These leads can be nurtured with targeted marketing campaigns to convert them into paying customers.

Build Brand Awareness:

A well-written book may aid in boosting your company's reputation and brand recognition. Promoting your book through social media, email marketing, and other channels can increase your visibility and reach new audiences.

Increase Speaking Engagements:

Authors with published books are often sought-after speakers for industry events and conferences. New commercial possibilities and collaborations may result from this.

Create New Products:

Your book's material can be used to create other products like podcasts, webinars, or online courses. This can generate additional revenue streams for your business.

Expand Your Network:

Writing a book can lead to new connections and partnerships with other professionals in your industry. New business possibilities and partnerships may result from this.

Boost Search Engine Optimization (SEO):

By optimizing your book's title, description, and other metadata, you can improve your website's SEO and increase your visibility in search results.

By leveraging your book for business growth, you can establish yourself as a thought leader, generate leads, increase brand awareness, create new products, expand your network, boost SEO, and ultimately grow your business.

CHAPTER 10
MEASURING SUCCESS

To assess your achievement, you must set objectives, but not all goals are created equal. Setting specific, measurable, attainable, pertinent, and time-bound goals can provide you the groundwork you need to gauge the success of your project.

What Success Looks Like

Success may take many different shapes, depending on the project you're presenting. Asking yourself what success looks like is a terrific approach to starting this process. You may move backward through the process to find the specifics that define your vision of success and the call to action to attain it if you already know what success looks like.

The metrics you use to gauge the performance of your book rely on the objectives you set for it. Here are several methods to measure your book's success:

Sales:

The number of book sales can measure success, primarily if your book generates a profit for your business.

Reviews:

Positive reviews and feedback from readers indicate that your book has resonated with its audience and has provided value to them.

Media coverage:

Reviews, interviews, and mentions in the media about your book may raise your profile and position you as a specialist in your field.

Speaking engagements:

The number of speaking engagements you are invited to can measure success, as it can indicate that your book has established you as an expert in your field.

Business opportunities:

The number of new business opportunities from your book, such as partnerships, collaborations, or consulting gigs, can indicate its success.

Email list growth:

The number of new subscribers to your email list can indicate the success of your book, as it shows that readers are interested in learning more from you.

Impact on readers:

The impact your book has had on readers can be a measure of success, significantly if it has helped them solve a problem, learn something new, or make positive changes in their lives.

Setting reasonable goals for your book and basing success on those goals is crucial. For example, some authors may prioritize sales, while others prioritize impact on readers or media coverage. Whatever your goals, tracking and analyzing data can help you determine what worked and what didn't and make adjustments for future books or business strategies.

Setting Success Metrics For Your Book

It is essential to establish success metrics for your book to assess the success or failure of your marketing plan and ensure you are meeting your objectives. The following stages will assist you in creating success measures for your book:

Define your goals:

Identifying the objectives for your book is the first stage. This can entail boosting your brand's visibility, generating leads, or establishing yourself as a thought leader in your field.

Identify your target audience:

Determine the target audience for your book and what they want to achieve from reading it. This will help you to identify key metrics that resonate with them.

Determine your key performance indicators (KPIs):

KPIs are specific metrics that measure the success of your marketing efforts. These could include book sales, website traffic, social media engagement, or email list growth.

Set realistic targets:

Set realistic targets for each KPI based on your goals, audience, and previous performance. Please make sure they are specific, measurable, and achievable.

Track and analyze your data:

Utilize analytics tools to monitor your KPIs and examine your data to determine what is impractical. This will help you to adjust your marketing strategy and optimize your efforts for maximum impact.

Adjust your strategy:

Use your data analysis to adjust your marketing strategy and make changes where necessary. Be prepared to test out many systems until you discover the ones that are most effective for your audience.

By setting success metrics for your book, you can better measure the impact of your marketing efforts and ensure that you are achieving your goals. This will assist you in maximizing the effectiveness of your plan and ensuring the success of both your book and your company.

Tracking Milestones

Tracking milestones is an integral part of measuring progress toward achieving your goals. Here are some steps to help you track milestones effectively:

Define your milestones:

The first step is to define the milestones you want to achieve. These should be specific and measurable goals aligned with your objectives.

Set a timeline:

Determine the timeframe for achieving each milestone. By doing this, you'll be able to stay on track and move closer to your goals.

Assign responsibility:

Assign responsibility for each milestone to a specific team member or department. This will assist in maintaining accountability and ensure that everyone knows their duties.

Monitor progress:

Monitor progress towards each milestone regularly to ensure you are on track. Utilize analytics and data technologies to monitor performance and identify potential issues that need fixing.

Adjust your strategy:

If you are not on track to achieve a milestone, adjust your strategy to get back on track. This may involve making changes to your approach or allocating additional resources.

Celebrate success:

When you achieve a milestone, celebrate your success with your team. This will build momentum and motivate everyone to work toward the next milestone.

Effective milestone tracking allows you to monitor your progress toward your objectives and make the required corrections to stay on course. As a result, your book and business will succeed due to your increased efficiency and effectiveness in achieving your goals.

Using Ai Analytics Tools To Measure Impact

Using AI analytics tools can be a powerful way to measure your book's impact and overall business goals. Here are some ways in which AI analytics tools can be used to measure impact:

Social media metrics:

AI analytics tools can help you measure engagement, such as likes, shares, comments, and followers. This may assist you in determining the amount of interest in your book and brand, as well as trends and potential improvement areas.

Website analytics:

AI tools can provide valuable insights into website traffic, user behavior, and engagement. This can assist you with website optimization and user experience improvement, which will eventually increase conversions and revenue.

Sales analytics:

AI tools can help you track sales performance, such as revenue, units sold, and conversion rates. This can assist you in determining which marketing tactics and channels work best to increase sales and make data-driven decisions to improve your sales success.

Customer feedback analytics:

AI tools can help you collect and analyze customer feedback, such as reviews, ratings, and survey responses. You may use this to understand client requirements and preferences better and find areas where your book and business can be improved. You may learn a lot about your book and your business as you make data-driven decisions that will enhance performance and reach your objectives by utilizing AI analytics tools to analyze the effect.

CHAPTER 11
CONTINUING YOUR JOURNEY
WITH AI

There are several methods you may use AI as you move forward with your AI journey to promote expansion and success in your company:

Automating repetitive tasks:

AI can help you automate tasks such as data entry, content creation, and customer service. Automating these operations might free up resources and time to devote to more essential functions that foster innovation and progress.

Enhancing customer experience:

AI can enhance customer experience by providing personalized recommendations, improving search functionality, and optimizing the user interface. As a result, you can improve client retention, loyalty, and happiness by giving them a better overall experience.

Predicting trends and patterns

AI can analyze data and predict trends and patterns in customer behavior, market trends, and other vital indicators. By leveraging these insights, you can make data-driven decisions and take proactive steps to stay ahead of the competition.

Optimizing marketing and advertising:

AI can optimize marketing campaigns by targeting specific audiences, identifying the most effective channels and messages, and measuring performance. By using AI in marketing and advertising, you may improve the efficiency of your campaigns, produce more leads, and boost sales.

AI can potentially transform into a very effective tool for the expansion and success of your business. By leveraging this technology, you can automate repetitive tasks, enhance customer experience, predict trends and patterns, and optimize marketing and advertising.

Keys To A Successful Business Book

The following essential components can contribute to the success of a business book:

Clear and Concise Writing:

A good business book should be written in simple, reader-friendly language that is straightforward and short. Avoid using technical or jargon terminology that can be hard for your audience to understand.

Unique and Compelling Angle:

A successful business book has to stand out from other books in its genre with a distinctive and captivating perspective. This may be a fresh take on an old subject or a brand-new notion.

Relevant and Timely Content:

A successful business book should address an appropriate and timely topic that interests your target audience. It should provide insights and solutions that are actionable and relevant to the challenges faced by your readers.

Engaging and Well-Structured Content:

A successful business book should be engaging and well-structured, with clear headings, subheadings, and chapters that guide the reader through the content. It should also include real-world examples, case studies, and anecdotes to illustrate key points.

Authentic and Personal Storytelling:

A successful business book should be precise and personal, with storytelling that resonates with readers. It should provide insights into the author's experiences and lessons learned and be relatable to readers.

High-Quality Design and Presentation:

A successful business book should be well-designed and professionally presented, with high-quality graphics and images that enhance the reader's experience. It should also be edited and proofread to ensure the content is error-free and easy to read.

Effective Marketing and Promotion:

A successful business book should be effectively marketed and promoted, with a strong online presence and targeted marketing campaigns that reach the right audience. Positive reviews and testimonials from readers should also support it.

You may improve the likelihood that your business book will be successful, make sure it adds value to readers, and support your company objectives by integrating five crucial components.

Looking Ahead To The Future Of Ai For Business

The future of AI for business is both exciting and challenging. On the one hand, AI can fundamentally alter how companies do business and make choices. But on the other hand, it can speed up decision-making for organizations, automate repetitive operations, and analyze enormous volumes of data to find patterns and insights.

On the other hand, the rapid growth of AI also poses new difficulties and moral dilemmas. For example, concerns exist over the possible effects of AI on employment and job displacement, as well as the dangers of bias in AI and the potential exploitation of AI for evil intentions.

Despite these challenges, the potential benefits of AI for business are significant. Here are a few domains where AI is probably going to become more effective in the future:

Personalization:

AI may assist companies in tailoring their goods and services to each customer's particular requirements and preferences. This can enhance customer experiences and increase customer loyalty.

Automation:

Routine jobs may be automated by AI, freeing up staff to concentrate on more challenging and strategic work. This can increase productivity and efficiency while also reducing costs.

Predictive Analytics:

AI can analyze enormous volumes of data to find patterns and forecast future trends and events. This can assist companies in making wiser decisions and retaining an advantage over rivals.

Cybersecurity:

AI can help businesses detect and respond to cyber threats in real time, improving overall security and reducing the risk of data breaches.

Sustainability:

AI can analyze enormous volumes of data to find patterns and forecast future trends and events. This can assist companies in making wiser decisions and retaining an advantage over rivals.

Businesses will need to keep current on new advancements and figure out how to responsibly and ethically integrate AI into their operations as AI technology develops and matures. It will be vital to continue investing in research, development, and training to ensure that AI is applied in a way that benefits both enterprises and society.

Are you prepared to use AI to advance your company? Become a member now to begin your path to exponential development. _Click this link here_... to get the materials and tools you need to succeed. Take advantage of this chance to modernize your company and stay ahead of the competition. _Join right away!_

Reference

- https://amt.land/2023/01/07/there-are-many-ways-that-artificial-intelligence-ai-can-be-used-to-improve-efficiency-and-productivity-in-the-workplace/
- https://differbtw.com/difference-between-business-strategy-and-corporate-strategy/
- https://nativeimmigration.com/tag/how-to-apply-for-student-visa-for-canada/
- https://saviorlabs.com/2023/01/04/how-to-choose-the-right-software-for-your-business-needs/
- https://www.angelfigueroamayordomo.com/training/team-lead
- https://dougbrownleadership.com/category/management/
- https://nashvillefitmagazine.com/2023-fitness-goals-are-they-reachable/
- https://www.handbid.com/blog/direct-mail-charity-auction-promotion
- https://arifriyanto.com/image-annotation/
- Lotz, C. (2014). Moving Things Around Safely. ISE ; Industrial and Systems Engineering at Work, 46(6), 34.
- https://lavender.solutions/mentoring/
- https://www.goodharboradvisors.com/p/investment-management
- https://www.job-hunt.org/how-to-prepare-for-a-job-search/
- https://performancein.com/news/2014/12/01/10-ways-improve-your-display-advertising-campaign/
- https://inside.6q.io/smart-goals-for-your-organisation/
- https://www.blog.flygenmedia.com/post/how-to-create-a-winning-brand-strategy
- https://www.claromentis.com/blog/developing-an-internal-communications-strategy/
- https://www.twoimpulse.com/industries/automotive
- https://www.blog.flygenmedia.com/post/how-to-create-a-winning-brand-strategy
- https://www.peoplemattersglobal.com/news/hr-technology/2021-singapore-hr-technology-market-map-29083

- https://kapitelh.de/leveraging-artificial-intelligence-and-machine-learning-to-automate-routine-processes-in-business/
- Michigan urges residents to spread fun, not germs. (2016, May 28). The Arab American News, 32(1581), 20.
- Michigan urges residents to spread fun, not germs. (2016, May 28). The Arab American News, 32(1581), 20.
- https://theannapolischiropractor.com/self-assessment-annapolis-md-chiropractor-dr-schwartz-chiropractic-adjustment-vertebrae-orthogonal/
- https://www.nowblitz.com/blog/real-estate-sales-training-7-tips-for-standout-success/
- https://www.limecube.co/8-ways-to-stand-out-in-a-crowded-market
- https://perfectionhangover.com/blog/
- https://writingstudio.com/blog/website-content/
- https://www.bluelilacmarketing.com/post/how-to-write-a-blog
- https://98bucksocial.com/blog/referral-traffic-using-facebook/
- https://kenmoo.me/b2b-video-marketing/
- https://98bucksocial.com/blog/referral-traffic-using-facebook/
- https://kenmoo.me/b2b-video-marketing/
- https://marketbrew.ai/creating-a-winning-content-marketing-strategy
- https://moss51.com/benefits-of-content-writing/
- https://stellapop.com/the-importance-of-authentic-and-connective-storytelling-in-branding/
- https://www.bol-agency.com/blog/best-account-based-marketing-email-examples
- https://www.restaurantmarketingservices.net/digital-marketing/pay-per-click-ads/
- https://marketomic.com/customer-retention-is-key-to-growth/

Author's Bio

Jennifer Branig is a business coach, public speaker, and coauthor of The best-selling book is called Aspire: Women Finding Their Purpose. The quickest way to write a book: Become a published author without paying a fortune, and also the author of the upcoming book:

When Life Sucks!
Stop Feeling Empty, Discover Your Why &
Live in Fulfilment Every Day

Jennifer has spent the last twenty years studying personal development, an education that has deeply impacted the businesses she has founded under the umbrella of Brasam Ltd.

Graduating from The Technical University of Berlin, in Germany, and working for The Berliner Sprachen Institute as a teacher, set Jennifer firmly on the road to coaching. For more than two decades, she has been committed to helping and encouraging vulnerable people and families towards living more fulfilling and satisfying lives.

Inspired by her work, she has transformed her deeply rooted vocation into Brasam Coaching Academy and Brasam Publishing of which she is the founder and owner. Today, Jennifer continues to help individuals and groups discover and fully embrace their life purpose through powerful online courses, dedicated counselling, and publishing services. Jennifer turns corporate professionals who have lost their identity through corporate conditioning into successful business owners.

She lives in London with her four children

Follow her on Facebook: _Jennifer Branig_

🌐 https://brasampublishinghouse.com/

✉️ jennifer@brasampublishinghouse.com

in www.linkedin/in/Jennifer-branig/

📷 @jenniferbranigbooks

Printed in Great Britain
by Amazon